What Shall We Pray About?

Andy Robb

Designed by Three's Company

Published in the U.S.A. by
Harvest House Publishers
Eugene, Oregon 97402

Library of Congress Cataloging-in-Publication Data

Robb, Andy
    What shall we pray about? / Andy Robb.
       p.   cm.
    Summary: Illustrations and simple text offer
suggestions to help children form their own prayers.
    ISBN 1-56507-753-9
    1. Prayer--Christianity--Juvenile literature.   [1. Prayer.]
I. Title.
BV212.R57 1998
248.3´2´0833--dc21   97-49680
                                                  CIP
                                                  AC

Worldwide coedition organised and produced by
Angus Hudson Ltd,
Concorde House, Grenville Place,
Mill Hill, London NW7 3SA, England
Tel: +44 181 959 3668
Fax +44 181 959 3678

Printed in Singapore

*For my two inspirations,
Matthew and Sarah*

Contents

What shall we pray about?

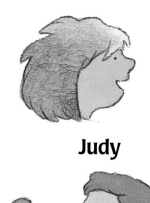

Judy

Pete

Ryan

Rajjan

Chelsea

Suggestions to pray about:
Thank God for your friends.

Sometimes our friends do things that upset us.
You can ask God to help you forgive them.

Our Friends

Andy

Bob

Su

Kurt

John

Do you know kids who have no friends?
Ask God to show you how you can be their friend.

Look at the picture and discover what else you can pray for.

What shall we pray about?

butterflies

clothing

fire

sun

jumping

music

wate[r]

electricity

books

food

computers

colors

Thank You For...

Suggestions to pray about:
Thank God for the sun that warms the earth and helps flowers grow. Thank God for the phone, so I can talk to my grandparents. Thank God for books to read that help me learn about people, places, and things.

night

home

clock

phone

smells

flowers

nature

fuel

wind

What shall we pray about?

dog

fish

magazine

vet

Suggestions to pray about:
A sick pet.

Thank God for the joy and fun that animals can bring us.

Animals

lion

cage

bone

mouse

bird

Thank God that we can play with the puppy.

Ask God to help us to care for all the animals He has made.

What shall we pray about?

pianist

baby

flowers

teacher

Suggestions to pray about:
Thank God for our minister.

Thank God for our Sunday school teachers.
Ask God to help us worship Him.

God's Family

minister

instruments

rainbow

offering bag

hat

Thank You for friends at church.

Thank You for new people at church. Help us welcome them.

What shall we pray about?

Rainy day

Snowy day

Sunny day

Suggestions to pray about:
For people in countries—hot and cold.

For animals in winter—that they can find food.

Whatever the Weather

Thank God for all the different sorts of weather.

Thank God for rainbows that remind us of His love for us.

What shall we pray about?

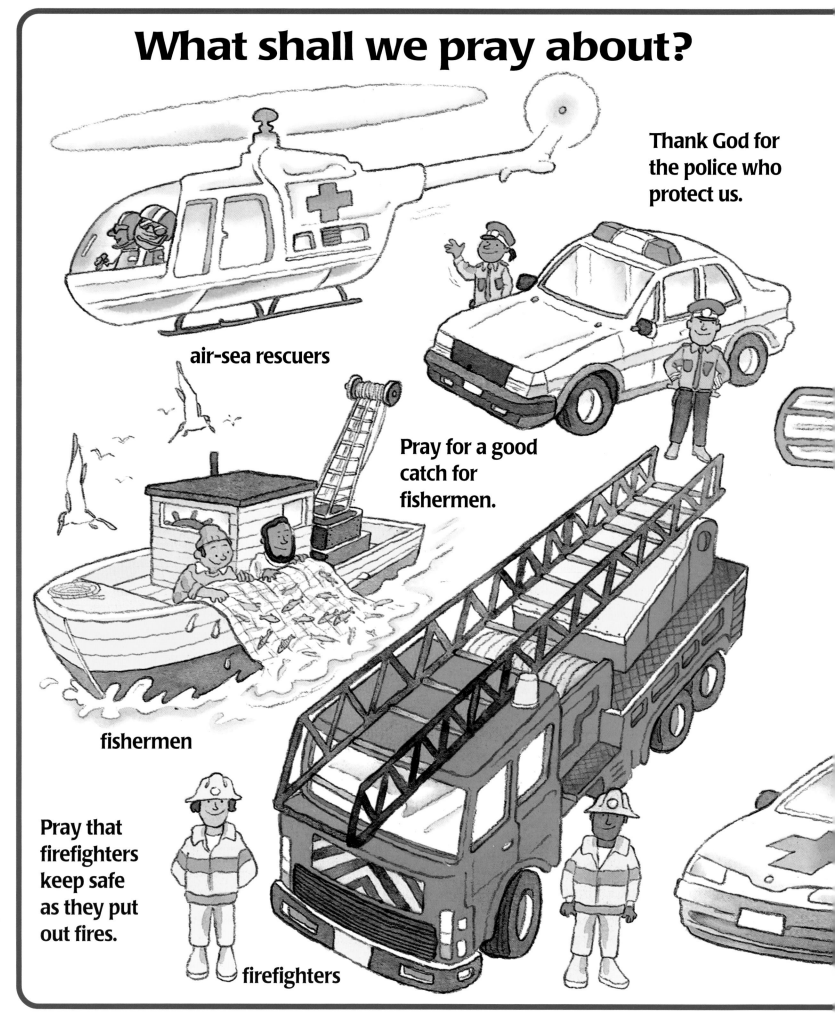

air-sea rescuers

Thank God for the police who protect us.

Pray for a good catch for fishermen.

fishermen

Pray that firefighters keep safe as they put out fires.

firefighters

People Who Help Us

truckers

farmers

Pray for good weather for the farmer's crops.

ambulance drivers

tow truck drivers

mail carriers

What shall we pray about?

Suggestions to pray about:

Peace in countries that are at war.

Children who live in all the countries of the world.

All Around the World

Ask God to give children everywhere enough to eat, a warm place to sleep, and people to love them and take care of them.

Thank God for all the different people in the world, and ask Him to help us to live together.

What shall we pray about?

Uncle

gift

drink

sister

Suggestions to pray about:
Help us get along with our brothers and sisters.

Thank God for our grandparents.

18

Families

Grandpa

camera

cat

cousin

Ask God to help us obey our parents and do what they ask without moaning.

People who haven't got families.

What shall we pray about?

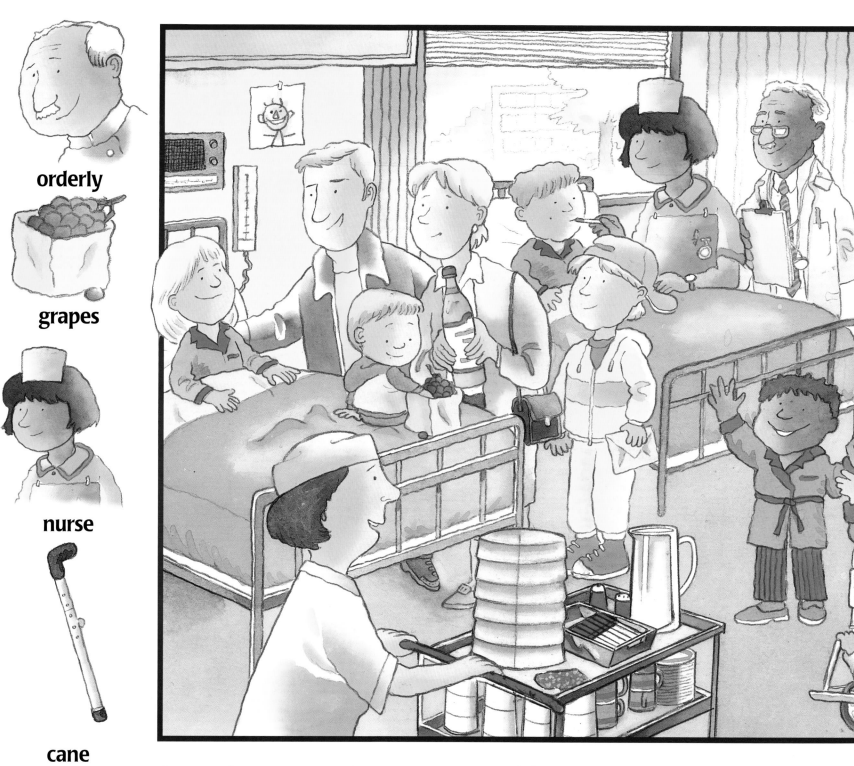

orderly

grapes

nurse

cane

Suggestions to pray about:
That doctors will know the best
treatment for sick friends or family
members.

Giving thanks for being well.

People Who Aren't Well

doctor

bandage

visitor

stethoscope

Pray for people without doctors and nurses.

Thank God for doctors, nurses, and dentists.

What shall we pray about?

new girl

chair

computer

naughty boy

Suggestions to pray about:
Sharing with others.

Ask God to help us listen to teachers,
and do what they say.

At School

teacher

pot

coat

helper

crayons

Learning new things.
Getting along with others.

Thank God for teachers.

What shall we pray about?

Suggestions to pray about:
Thank God that He is always with us.

For God's peace when we are worried.

When We Are Afraid

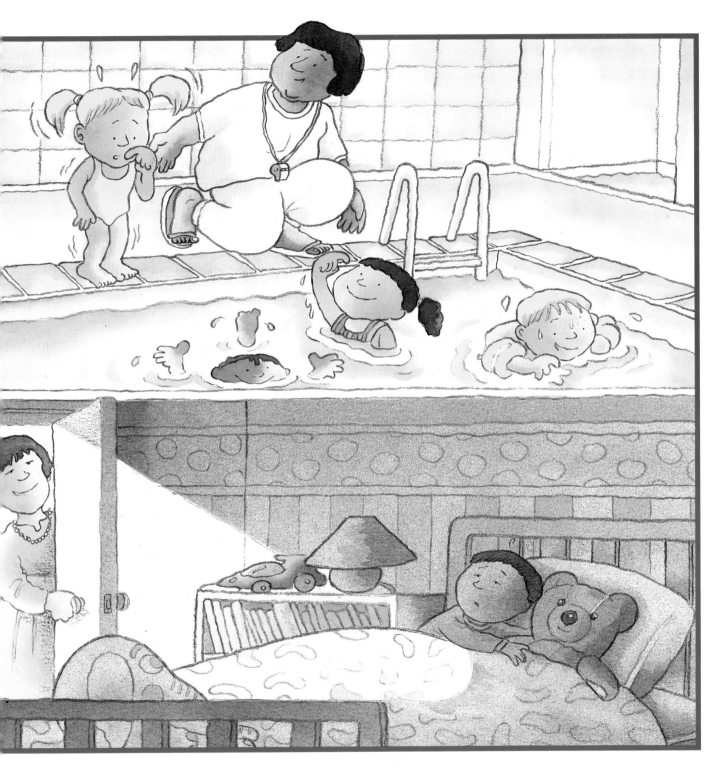

For protection when we are in trouble.

For help to do things we find hard.

What shall we pray about?

Grandma

cake

burger

boy

Suggestions to pray about:
Thank God for the fun of parties.

Thank God for the presents people give us.

Special Times

lady

car

balloon

friend

Ask God to help us share our special times with people who haven't got many friends.

Thank God for the excitement and fun we can have.

What shall we pray about?

Suggestions to pray about:

Thank God for Jesus.

Thank Jesus that He loves us.

Why not tell Jesus how much you love Him?

God's Love

Ask God to help us learn more about Jesus from the Bible.

What shall we pray about?

Suggestions to pray about:
Help us to share what we
have with others.

Sharing

Praying

Caring

Doing things
for others

Protecting

Sharing God's Love

Thank God that we can pray for our friends.

Ask God to help us put other people's needs before our own.

Being kind

Saying sorry

Thinking of others

Helping

What shall we pray about?

"It's amazing how many of my friends don't pray with their parents, even though they're all Christians," said a student. For teenagers, family praying is often embarrassing.

What can we do to change this?

Get used to praying

The best cure is prevention, starting with babies and toddlers. Kids should grow up knowing that praying together is as natural as breathing—praying together at any time, anywhere, about anything, and praying not just with parents but with grannies, uncles, and babysitters.

This is a habit that can be learned. And this book will help.

When shall we pray?

Not only in the morning, when you're looking forward to the day; not only at night, when you want to relax and thank God for the day; but also during the day, when kids are feeling fed up, or frazzled, or wondering what to do next. At moments like that you can pick up this book and pray and talk about the pictures. It will help you to see that praying together is interesting and lightens even dull and difficult moments.

What shall we pray about?

If we sit down and ask, "What shall we pray about?" our minds often go blank. The lambs? The pretty flowers? Children with nowhere to live? It can get boring.

Talking about the pictures in this book will spark ideas. The questions at the foot of some of the pages give some suggestions for talking points—but don't limit yourself to these.

On some pages, many things are happening—fun things and serious things. On other pages, there are many interesting objects. Ask what there is to see. Point to pictures on the page and ask what's happening,

Some scenes may remind small children of things that have happened to them that they forgot to tell you. The pictures may help them describe things they have experienced. But they may not. It doesn't matter. There should be no feeling of compulsion as you look at the pages.

Learning to read

Praying together, telling stories together, reading together, and learning new things together are part of one whole. As children read this book with you, they learn to link every part of their lives with Jesus.

One of the most important prereading and early reading gifts you can give is the feeling that books are fun, even adventurous, and tell you useful things. These pictures are interesting to look at and talk about.

A major prereading skill is being able to look with attention at shapes and outlines on a page, noting small details. As you talk about the pictures, this will happen automatically.

For kids to enjoy learning to read, it helps if they like the sounds and meanings of words and have enjoyed learning the names of things in a companionable atmosphere. Talk about the objects and parts of objects on the pages, giving their names. Talk about what they look like, their colors, and

how big they are. Imitate the sounds they make. Talk about what people might be saying.

Slowly small children come to understand that squiggly black lines—letters and words—have meanings and sounds. Slowly they learn to recognize words as you point to them and say them aloud. As reading skills grow, you could try sounding out the letters and reading some of the words together, but only if your child is interested.

Sing or say rhymes or songs about objects and ideas in the pictures. Adapt simple songs that you know, making up your own words. Songs such as "The wheels on the bus go round and round," and "Here we go round the mulberry bush" are very adaptable.

Stories open doors of understanding

Everybody loves stories, grown-ups as well as children. And books have a great advantage over the television—you can turn to the same picture over and over again. You can stay with it and find out more things about it.

If you make up simple stories about events in the pictures, children will love it. Ask: What's that boy doing? What's that girl thinking? What will she do next? What will her mom say or do? What's the name of that dog? That goose? How will it all end?

And your stories can be turned into prayer—prayer that is not a boring ritual, but a conversation with Jesus. Prayer that has meaning and understanding because it is based on feelings and events that you've talked about together.